THE GREAT OUTDOORS!

Water Sports

Mason Crest

THE GREAT OUTDOORS!

Camping

Discovering Nature

Fishing

Hiking and Backpacking

Horseback Riding

Hunting

Mountain Biking

Snow Sports

Survival Skills

Water Sports

Water Sports

DIANE BAILEY

Mason Crest
450 Parkway Drive, Suite D
Broomall, PA 19008
www.masoncrest.com

© 2017 by Mason Crest, an imprint of National Highlights, Inc.

All rights reserved. No part of this publication may be reproduced or transmitted in any form or by any means, electronic or mechanical, including photocopying, recording, taping, or any information storage and retrieval system, without permission from the publisher.

Printed and bound in the United States of America.

Series ISBN: 978-1-4222-3565-2
Hardback ISBN: 978-1-4222-3575-1
EBook ISBN: 978-1-4222-8320-2

First printing
1 3 5 7 9 8 6 4 2

Produced by Shoreline Publishing Group LLC
Santa Barbara, California
Editorial Director: James Buckley Jr.
Designer: Patty Kelley
Production: Sandy Gordon
www.shorelinepublishing.com

Cover photographs by Galina Barskaya/Dreamstime.com.

Names: Bailey, Diane, 1966-
Title: Water sports / by Diane Bailey.
Description: Broomall, PA : Mason Crest, [2017] | Series: The Great
    Outdoors | Includes index.
Identifiers: LCCN 2016008710| ISBN 9781422235751 (Hardback) | ISBN
 9781422235652 (Series) | ISBN 9781422283202 (eBook)
Subjects: LCSH: Aquatic sports--Juvenile literature.
Classification: LCC GV770.5 .B35 2017 | DDC 797--dc23
LC record available at http://lccn.loc.gov/2016008710

QR CODES AND LINKS TO THIRD PARTY CONTENT
You may gain access to certain third party content ("Third Party Sites") by scanning and using the QR Codes that appear in this publication (the "QR Codes"). We do not operate or control in any respect any information, products or services on such Third Party Sites linked to by us via the QR Codes included in this publication, and we assume no responsibility for any materials you may access using the QR Codes. Your use of the QR Codes may be subject to terms, limitations, or restrictions set forth in the applicable terms of use or otherwise established by the owners of the Third Party Sites. Our linking to such Third Party Sites via the QR Codes does not imply an endorsement or sponsorship of such Third Party Sites, or the information, products or services offered on or through the Third Party Sites, nor does it imply an endorsement or sponsorship of this publication by the owners of such Third Party Sites.

CONTENTS

Chapter 1: Into the Great Outdoors! 6
Chapter 2: Getting It Done Right 14
Chapter 3: Get Great Gear 26
Chapter 4: Further Adventures 36
Find Out More. 46
Series Glossary of Key Terms 47
Index/Author 48

KEY ICONS TO LOOK FOR

Words to Understand: These words with their easy-to-understand definitions will increase the reader's understanding of the text, while building vocabulary skills.

Sidebars: This boxed material within the main text allows readers to build knowledge, gain insights, explore possibilities, and broaden their perspectives by weaving together additional information to provide realistic and holistic perspectives.

Research Projects: Readers are pointed toward areas of further inquiry connected to each chapter. Suggestions are provided for projects that encourage deeper research and analysis.

Text-Dependent Questions: These questions send the reader back to the text for more careful attention to the evidence presented here.

Series Glossary of Key Terms: This back-of-the-book glossary contains terminology used throughout this series. Words found here increase the reader's ability to read and comprehend higher-level books and articles in this field.

Educational Videos: Readers can view videos by scanning our QR codes, providing them with additional educational content to supplement the text. Examples include news coverage, moments in history, speeches, iconic sports moments and much more!

CHAPTER 1

Into the Great Outdoors!

hen the weather heats up, lots of people can't wait to jump in the water and splash around. It doesn't take much planning to put on a swimsuit and blow up a beach ball. But there are some people who like to bump things up a notch. They stay cool by grabbing their skis and sails, hooking up to their boats and boards, and heading out for some *serious* water fun.

Swimming is a water sport that's just about using your body. Others, like boating, are more about technical skills and equipment. Then there are some that are the

 WORDS TO UNDERSTAND

aerial in the air

fiberglass a type of plastic strengthened with small threads of glass

wake the waves produced by the movement of a boat

perfect balance between the two. Maybe you're a chill surfer, your toes gripping your board as you ride the curl of a wave to shore. Maybe you're an adventurous windsurfer, letting the wind lift you off the surface of the water. Or maybe you're a thrill-seeker, getting a rush as you zip through the water at 30 miles (48 km) per hour on water skis or a wakeboard.

Whatever your style, many basic skills can be picked up quickly and used in a variety of water sports. With the sun on your back and a spray of water in your face, they are an exciting way to get outside. Get ready to dive in!

Getting in Deep

Water sports have been around for thousands of years. In the last century, they have gotten a lot more sophisticated. The first surfers probably just used their bodies to ride the waves. Next they climbed on top of a wooden board. This let them float longer and catch even larger waves. By the 1400s, surfing was a royal sport. The tribal kings of Hawaii had surfing competitions to show their strength and power.

Surfing fell out of fashion for a while, but it started to get popular again in the early 1900s. By the 1930s, surfing was getting some big improvements. People tried different shapes of boards. They added fins on the bottom of the boards to help them steer. Instead of wood, they tried lighter materials, such as foam. Later they used **fiberglass**. Surfing was developing into a modern sport.

Some people like to try big-wave surfing. This is much more difficult than regular surfing. The waves can be 20 feet (6 m) tall or more. The biggest wave ever surfed (so far!) is 78 feet (23.8 m)!

Surfers and sailors have always shared the water. By the 1960s the two sports were beginning to merge. Using a sail attached to a surfboard, people combined the skills of sailing and surfing into a new sport called windsurfing. Windsurfing is also called sailboarding. Some windsurfers say the sport is less like sailing or surfing than it is like

For many people, water skiing is the most accessible water sport.

flying. Windsurfers often get enough air that they can rise several feet over the water. A similar sport is kiteboarding, where, instead of a sail, the board is powered by a high-flying kite that catches the wind.

Give it Some Gas

Water sports really took off in the 20th century. The gasoline engine had been invented. It made going fast much easier. Regular boats became motorboats! People did not have to depend on the wind or their muscles to move through the water. Instead, they had a much more reliable and powerful source of energy. It was

SKIP THE SKIS

Want to try water skiing without skis? That's what barefooters do. They still get pulled by a boat, but they use their bare feet to skim through the water. It takes faster speeds to stay up on bare feet, because there is less surface area to float on the water. The boats usually go about 40 miles (63 km) per hour. Barefooting can be pretty hard on the feet, but these athletes are tough. If they get a cut, they just use fast-acting glue to patch it up. Just as in regular water skiing, barefooters also do tricks and jumps. Professionals can jump 90 feet (27.4 m) or more!

fun to ride in a boat zipping along at 25 miles (40 km) an hour, but it might be even more fun to ride behind it. If it was possible to ski on snow, then why not on water?

   In 1922, a teenager named Ralph Samuelson decided to give it a try. He made some water skis using pieces of wood from barrels. Then his brother pulled him behind a boat on a lake in Minnesota, where they lived. A few years later, Ralph also performed a ski jump in the water.

He even tried speed skiing, reaching 80 miles (129 km) per hour! Water skiing caught on. Today, about 20 million people in the United States enjoy water skiing.

Wakeboarding combines water skiing and surfing. When a motorboat cuts through the water, it churns it up into a **wake**. Wakeboarders then ride through these waves on a board. A wakeboard is similar to a surfboard or snowboard, but shorter and wider. It's also possible to be towed from an overhead cable. Several high towers are installed at various points around a lake. Then cables are strung between them to pull riders. The big difference with cables is that there is no boat to create a wake. This makes a different—but no less fun—kind of ride. For example, cable wakeboarders have the advantage of having extra lift provided by the cable. That makes it easier to do tricks.

Getting Your Feet Wet

You can't do water sports without water, but that does not mean you have to live just a few steps from the ocean. Water skiing, wakeboarding, and windsurfing can all be done on lakes. Some large lakes even have good-sized waves for surfers. Also, many larger cities now have indoor wave pools. In those, machines create the surf. Indoor surfing isn't the same experience as being in the ocean. Still, it's great for extra practice or when it's cold outside.

Most water sports are individual, not team, sports. However, water skiing and wakeboarding are at least two-person jobs. Someone has to drive the boat! Pulling a skier or boarder requires certain skills, so it's important to get someone with experience. The quality of the pull can mean the difference between a good run and a bad one. Fortunately, there are many places at beaches and lakes that rent equipment, offer lessons, and have people to operate the boat.

It's not necessary to be a star athlete to try water sports. People who are reasonably fit with average strength should have what it takes. They just won't be trying **aerial** tricks or tackling 30-foot (9 m) waves—not at first, anyway!

This surfer is ready for action with a wetsuit, helmet, and leash.

The most important thing to consider with water sports is safety. It's likely that the first few times you try a new water sport, you won't get it quite right. Even though these sports are done on the water, you'll probably spend quite a bit of time in it. You'll fall off the skis or board. The surf will go over your head instead of under your feet. It's important to be comfortable in the water. If you do not know how to swim, that's the first thing to learn. Also, always wear a life vest, and never attempt to try something alone. Always take a buddy so you can watch out for each other.

TEXT-DEPENDENT QUESTIONS

1. What two sports are combined in windsurfing?

2. Besides using a boat, what is another way to enjoy wakeboarding?

3. Why do barefoot water skiers have to go faster?

 ## RESEARCH PROJECT

Surfing is one of the oldest water sports. Wakeboarding is one of the newest. Pick your favorite water sport and look up its history. What are some of the major milestones in its development?

Try Barefoot Water Skiing!

CHAPTER 2

Getting It Done Right

f you asked someone who is experienced at water sports for some tips, you might get the answer: "Know what you're getting into." One of the best ways to do that is to take a lesson or two. Spending a little time up front can save you a lot of time later on. A professional can point out what you're doing wrong, and give you advice on how to fix it. That way, you don't waste hours making the same mistakes.

 WORDS TO UNDERSTAND

kit all the parts of a windsurfing craft, including the board, sail, mast, and other equipment

planing skimming across the surface of the water at a high speed

rip current a powerful current that flows away from the shore

throttle a device that controls how much gas goes into an engine

15

Before entering the water, observe the conditions of wind, wave, and tide.

Before You Go

You've put on your swimsuit (or your wetsuit) and stocked a cooler with drinks and snacks. Don't hit the water just yet, though. Take some time to watch it first. If you are surfing, note how big the waves are. What direction are they coming from? Where are they breaking?

Windsurfers will need to know what direction the wind is coming from, and how hard it's blowing. A steady breeze is ideal, but that does not always happen. A hard, gusting wind can easily blow a beginner off course. It also can produce large waves that are hard to handle. On the other hand, if there is no wind at all you might get stranded!

If you're water skiing or wakeboarding, the power of the boat will help you along, but it's still important to consider the water conditions. Calm water will give you a much different ride than a choppy surface.

Things going on below the surface of the water are hard to see, but they can also be dangerous. **Rip currents** in the ocean can pull people far away from the shore, out into deep water. They can overwhelm even strong, experienced swimmers. Rip currents are affected by the weather, and can form quickly. One sign of a possible rip current is when a horizontal line of waves has a gap in between them. That can mean that the water is flowing back to the ocean, instead of toward the shore with the rest of the waves.

Watch for signs that let you know about offshore conditions you might not see.

This surfer rides regular-foot as she carves into a turn.

Take a Stand

If you have ever stood up in a small boat, you know how hard it is to keep your balance. Even calm water moves a little bit—and sometimes it feels like a lot! It takes some time to adjust. Balancing on a board or skis is even more challenging. For one thing, there is less room to stand. Also, the smaller surface area makes the movement of the water seem stronger. Whether you are surfing, wind-surfing, water skiing or wakeboarding, getting your "sea legs" is one of the most important skills to master.

The first thing to figure out is where to put your feet. On a surfboard or wakeboard, most people put their left foot toward the front. They are "regular-foot" riders. Others are "goofy-footers." They prefer to have the right foot forward. Being able to ride either way is called "switch-foot." It can be a great advantage to ride switch-foot!

To get into a standing position, surfers use a move called a "pop up." First they lie on their stomachs, with their heads and shoulders raised. They grab the sides of the board with their hands, and their feet are flexed so their toes are gripping the board. Now, go! In one fast, fluid motion, they jump into a standing position. Their feet are now pointing to the long side of the board.

Standing up on water skis or a wakeboard takes different skills. In these sports, skiers and boarders have their feet strapped in. They let the power of the boat pull them up. To start out, the body will be mostly in the water. The knees are bent up to your chest, in a cannonball position. The arms are stretched straight out in front, holding the handle of the rope. Skiers will be sitting on the backs of their skis, which are underwater. The front edges are poking out. A wakeboard will have one of its long edges in the water, and the other long edge sticking out at a diagonal.

PADDLING OUT

For surfers, a big challenge is to get out to the waves. The bigger the wave, the farther out it is in the water. That means a lot of paddling. Surfers lie on their stomachs and paddle with their hands cupped together to push the water back. When a wave comes in, they want to make sure it doesn't hit them in the face or push them back into shore. One way to avoid it is to do a duck dive. For this, they shift their weight forward and push the nose (front) of the board under the wave. The wave will wash over them. That way, they won't find themselves back where they started!

When the boat starts to move, there are three main things to remember. One: keep your arms straight out in front of you. Two: make sure your knees are loose and slightly bent. Three: look up and forward—not down at your feet! As the boat gains speed, you might feel an urge to pull yourself into a standing position. Instead, keep your weight centered over your feet, and let the boat do the work. As it gently pulls you forward, use your leg muscles to stand up smoothly.

Turn it Around

Where do you want to go? Chances are, it's not right in front of you! Water doesn't move in a straight line, and neither should you. Whatever sport you're doing, you will want to be able to steer into and out of the waves to get the best ride. Turning is done through a series of small movements that shift your body weight and use the edges of your skis or board to carve through the water.

On a surfboard, surfers start with their upper bodies. Whichever foot is forward, they use the same arm to point where they want to go. So, a regular-foot rider, who has the left forward, will lead into a turn with the left arm (even if it's a right turn). The shoulders and hips will naturally follow until the body is pointed in the right direction. Then, he shifts his weight more to the edge of the surfboard to push it the same way.

Turning on a wakeboard is similar, but there's one major difference: you can't move your feet! A wakeboarder's feet are strapped into boots attached to the board, pointing toward one of the long sides. For a wakeboarder, the two sides of the board are called the toe-side and the heel-side. The body is facing mostly sideways on the board, but is slightly twisted toward the nose. To turn, a wakeboarder shifts his weight slightly onto either his heels or his toes, to move his board in the same direction. For a regular-foot rider, a heel-side turn will cause the board to move to the left. Using the rope is another important element in turning. Pulling on the rope creates tension, and that power helps move the board.

On a single water ski, turning calls for leaning on one edge.

To turn on a pair of skis, lean in the direction you want to go, but put more pressure on the opposite ski. So, if you want to turn right, lean slightly to the right, release some of the weight on your right ski, and press down on the inside edge of the left ski.

A boat is always creating a wake that the skier or boarder goes through. It makes a fun ride to turn into these waves and go through them. However, if you don't handle them correctly, it can get pretty bumpy. When turning through the wake, position the skis or board at a sharp angle to the wake, and keep your knees loose to absorb the impact of the waves.

21

IN THE DRIVER'S SEAT

Giving a rider a good "pull" is the job of a driver. Drivers must keep the boat at a consistent speed, especially when the skier or boarder is just standing up. As the rider comes through a wake, good drivers ease up on the **throttle** a bit to match the rider's speed. If the rider falls, the driver has to cut the throttle immediately and then gently circle back to pick him up. It's important not to make a high-speed return. This will just create more big waves that roll back onto the rider—and he's already wet enough!

Sail Away

Windsurfing takes surfing to a whole other level. A windsurfer must be able to control his body and manage a mini-sailboat—at the same time. The first step is to assemble the **kit**. This consists of the board (the part you stand on) and the rig (the sailing mechanism). First, the sail slides onto the mast, the tall pole that holds it up. Then the base of the mast is fitted onto the board. The boom is a horizontal bar that fits around the sail. The sailor holds onto the boom and uses it to maneuver the sail.

When everything is put together, it's time to get in the water, climb on the board, and pull up the sail. This can be hard work, depending on where the wind is coming from. Once it's up, though, things get easier. Now you can maneuver the rig.

A big goal of windsurfers is **planing**. The plane is the surface of the water. Most boats do not really travel on top of the water. They travel through it, with some of the boat underneath the surface. However, a fast motorboat will actually lift out of the water and skim across the top. Windsurfers can do this too if they get up enough speed.

To catch the wind, sailors use the boom to move the sail into or out of the wind. By controlling how much wind they get, they can adjust the speed of the sailboard. To turn, they use two basic moves: tacking and jibing. Tacking is positioning the front of the sailboard to move into the wind. Jibing is the opposite—pushing the back of the craft into the wind. Sailors use a combination of the two to travel forward in a zig-zag line.

A harness connects the windsurfer to the boom of the sail.

23

WHAT'S SUP?!

The hottest new water sport combines surfing, kayaking, and . . . standing? Stand-up paddleboarding, known as SUP, uses a wide, flat board that usually has a rubber mat for standing on. Riders climb on and balance with their feet apart pointing straight ahead. Then they use a long paddle to guide themselves through the water. SUP boards are great on lakes as well as near beaches on calm days. Tourists love them when visiting beach cities. The view while standing gives a different perspective then while sitting on a kayak. Expert riders can paddle the boards into waves and ride the paddleboard like a surfboard, though not with as much ability to do tight turns. The work of paddling the board while balancing with your body and your legs also means that SUP is a full-body workout. If you exercise too much, you can just jump off the board for a cooling dip in the water before climbing back on!

Stand-up paddleboarding calls for good balance, but it's a great workout.

TEXT-DEPENDENT QUESTIONS

1. How are rip currents dangerous?
2. Which foot does a regular-foot rider put forward?
3. How does a windsurfer use the boom?

 RESEARCH PROJECT

Watching experienced athletes is a good way to pick up tips. Choose a sport and watch videos of how the experts do different moves.

Windsurfing: Learning How to Start from the Beach

CHAPTER 3

Get Great Gear

etting good at any sport means learning the right skills and practicing them a lot. To make sure you're getting the most out of your hard work, it's important to have good equipment. When you are first trying out a new sport, start with renting some basic equipment. This lets you experiment with different sizes and styles. You can determine what works best for you. Once you've been out on the water several times, you'll have a better idea of what you like.

 WORDS TO UNDERSTAND

gun a long, fast surfboard

rocker the amount of curve in skis or a board

slalom a course that involves sharp turns around a series of obstacles

Renting is a great option for the occasional Saturday at the beach. However, if you really get into a sport and start doing it every Saturday, you'll probably want your own stuff. That will cost less over time. Plus, you can get exactly what you want. Buying gear can get expensive fast. Fortunately, it's not necessary to spend your life savings right at the beginning. Only expert athletes really need the highest-end boards or skis. If you're still learning the ropes and just out for some fun, more affordable gear will be fine.

Size and Shape

Skis and boards come in different lengths, widths, and thicknesses. They have different overall shapes and are made of a variety of materials. With so many choices, it can be tough to make the right decision!

Water skiers have two choices: one ski or two. Most water skiers start out on a pair of combo skis—one for each foot. After they get better, they can move on to using a single ski called a slalom ski. These are more difficult to use, but faster and more versatile.

A few factors go into choosing the right skis. Your height and weight, your style of skiing, and how fast you plan to ski all are things to consider. Longer skis are slower and more stable, so they are good for beginners. Also, skis sink more easily when they are moving slowly. Beginners usually need a wider ski to help them float at slower speeds. More advanced skiers can move onto skis that are narrower and faster. They might also have a bigger curve on the bottom. This helps with turning and tricks.

Surfers and wakeboarders will have to choose a board that's the right size. Experienced surfers sometimes use a long narrow board called a gun. These can be 13 feet (4 m) long. They are good for gaining speed and paddling into big waves. The long edge, or rail, lets the surfer zip through the water. A beginning surfer will probably want a slightly shorter, lighter board. A good rule of thumb is to get a board that is six inches to a foot (.15m to .3 m) longer than your height.

The type of water ski you choose will depend on your ability level and type of skiing.

Wakeboards are kind of like surfboards, with a little bit of snowboard and skateboard thrown in. As with surfboards, it's important to get one that matches your size, experience level, and style. Short boards are good for tricks and sharp moves in the water, but they are harder to learn on.

Surfers choose the right size, shape, and weight for their boards.

Fins and Rockers

Besides the overall size and shape, there are other things that affect how skis and boards perform in the water. Most skis and boards are slightly curved, so that the two ends stick up just a little bit more than the middle. This is known as the **rocker**. The amount of rocker determines how much of the skis or board touch the water at any given time. In general, less rocker means that more surface area comes into contact with the water. That offers more control. More rocker means less control—but it also means riders can go faster and make sharper turns.

Another thing to consider is fins. Fins are attached to the bottom of the board or skis. As the rider shifts his weight in one direction or the other, the fins push against the water to help in the turn. The number, size, and placement of the fins all produce a different "feel." Riders can customize them just the way they like. Beginners usually choose longer, deeper fins. They help grab the water and add stability. More advanced riders usually want smaller fins. These riders need a little bit of control, but they also want to be able to turn quickly and easily.

Materials

Several different materials are used to make skis and boards. Wood was the original material, but it warps easily and wears out quickly. Now manufacturers use more advanced materials, such as foam, fiberglass, graphite, and carbon fiber.

Many surfboards and wakeboards are made with a thin inner layer of foam or wood, surrounded by layers of fiberglass. The fiberglass gives a rigid feel, but it works with the inner core to help manage the flexibility. Flexibility is not good or bad—it just depends on what a rider wants. A more flexible board is easier to manage, and absorbs bumps better. A stiffer board is just the opposite. Instead of absorbing the impact, it will bounce off the wave. Advanced riders often like stiffer boards because they can catch more air.

Fiberglass has also been a big improvement to skis, which used to be made of wood or aluminum. Fiberglass makes skis much more durable and flexible. However, fiberglass is heavier and harder to manage, which is especially noticeable in skis. Some skis combine fiberglass and a lightweight material called graphite. This helps with the weight, while still keeping the skis fast and flexible. These types of skis are particularly good for speed skiing and jumping, where every inch counts! Another material is carbon fiber. It is very light, very flexible—and very expensive. It's used in high-end equipment for professionals.

STRAPPED IN

Stay together—with your skis or board, that is. When you're skimming through the water at 30 miles (48 km) per hour, you definitely want to stay buckled in. Water skiers and wakeboarders wear a combination of a boot and a binding. The boot part is made of a soft material that fits snugly around your foot. It holds you in place and helps transfer power from your body to your feet. The bindings attach the boot to the ski, but they also have a special release mechanism. If you fall, they are designed to snap out to prevent an injury.

Sailboards

Windsurfers need a board, a sail, and the equipment that connects the two. Beginning windsurfers should choose a larger board for more stability. Beginner boards also come with a daggerboard, a smaller board that thrusts down from the bottom of the board, into the water. A daggerboard adds stability. It also helps the board perform even in very light wind.

More advanced windsurfers can use a shorter board called a freeride board. It combines speed with maneuverability. From there, a windsurfer might try a slalom board, which is even smaller, lighter, and faster. A speed board is the fastest type. They work well only when the wind is strong.

There are several things to think about when choosing a sail. First, what size board do you have? A larger board needs a larger sail. Also consider the type of wind conditions. If the wind is very strong, a smaller sail will still catch a lot of wind. If the winds are gentle, you'll probably need a bigger sail.

Another thing to consider is your style of sailing. If you are sailing in heavy winds and big waves, then a wave sail is a good idea. These are smaller than other sails, and more durable. Even though the waves are slapping at them all the time, they won't wear out too fast. On the other hand, a slalom sail is much bigger. They are used for racing. There

A windsurfing thrill: "Catching air" while jumping over an oncoming wave.

WETSUITS

Seventy degrees sounds perfect, right? Not if that's the water temperature! It's easy to get cold—fast—in water that's less than about 75 to 80 degrees F (24 to 26 degrees C). A wetsuit can help hold your body heat in. Most wetsuits are made of neoprene. Neoprene is a type of man-made rubber that is flexible and very good at insulation. Choose a wetsuit that's rated for the water temperature that you'll be in. Thicker wetsuits will keep you warm even in very cold water. They also use a different type of stitching that prevents too much water from seeping in. However, they'll be heavier and bulkier. A lighter wetsuit will do the job in water that's not extremely cold.

is more surface area to go fast even in light wind. These sails are also lighter, but the tradeoff is that they are more delicate. It's easier to damage them. A freeride sail is good for general use. They are a good combination of being fast and easy to use.

Whatever sport you pick, remember that having advanced gear only helps if you know how to use it. When you are just starting out, choose equipment that matches your ability level. That will make learning the sport easier.

TEXT-DEPENDENT QUESTIONS

1. How do fins help control skis or a board?

2. Why would a rider want a board that is rigid and less flexible?

3. What are some characteristics of a race, or slalom, sail?

RESEARCH PROJECT

Are you into speed? Tricks? Whichever sport you want to pursue, think about what your style would be. Now, research the kind of equipment you would need for that.

The Basics of Surfboard Design

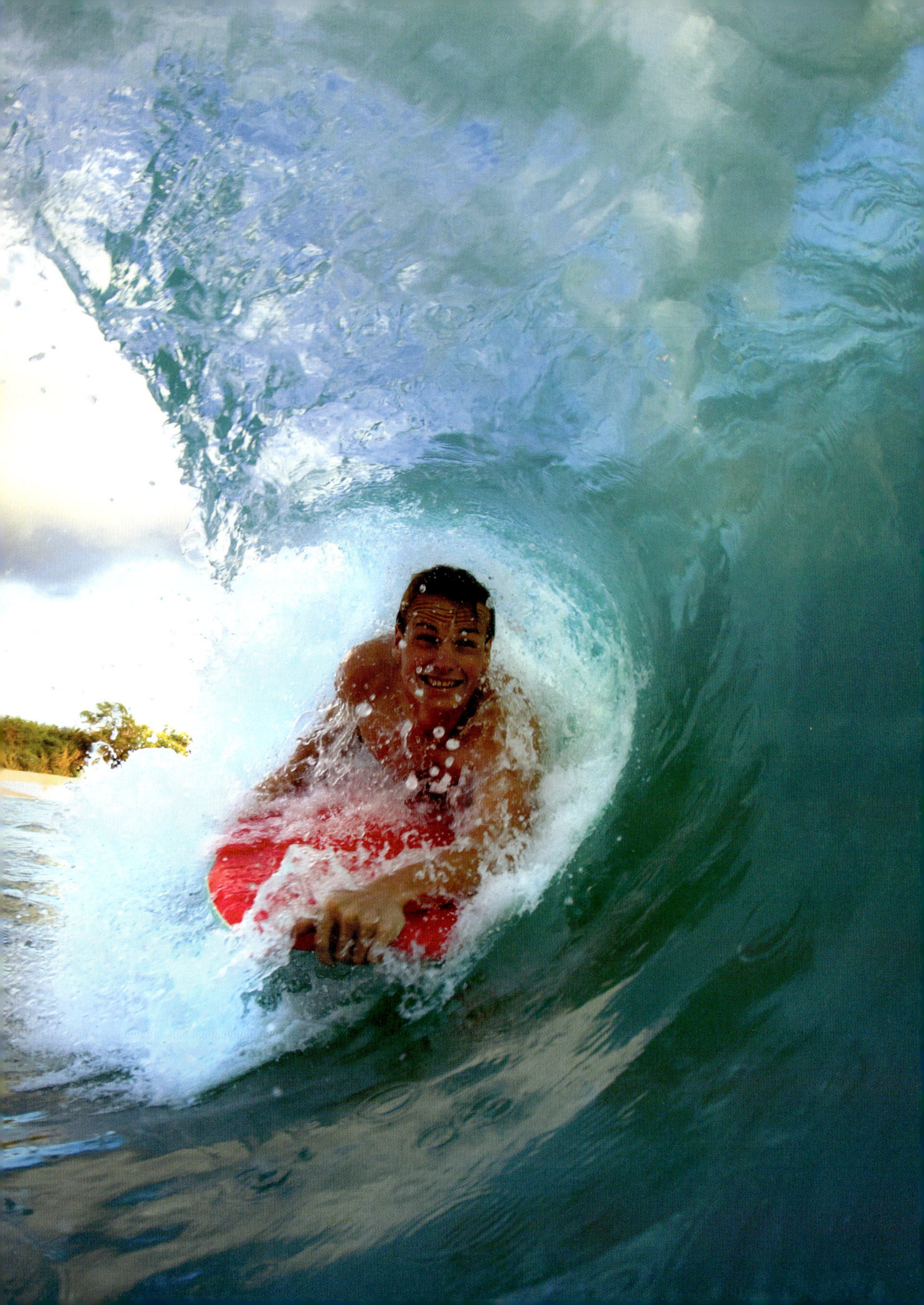

CHAPTER 4

Further Adventures

There are more than 700,000 miles (1,126,541 km) of ocean coastline in the world, and even more if you add in rivers and lakes. All together, they surround trillions upon trillions of gallons of water. That's a lot to choose from! So where's the best place to go enjoy water sports? That all depends on your sport and your style.

WORDS TO UNDERSTAND

buoy an object that floats in the water and serves as a marker

continental the U.S. mainland, not including Alaska and Hawaii

precision a large amount of detail and exactness

Believe it or not, this surfer is riding a wave on Lake Michigan!

Pick Your Spot

Surfing is one of the oldest water sports around. People in Polynesia and Hawaii have been doing it for centuries. The water there is warm, and there are lots of different water conditions to choose from—gentle surf to monster waves. In the **continental** United States, some surfers like the east coast and some like the west. In general, the west coast has bigger, smoother waves. East coast waters are choppier, but that's a challenge some surfers like. There's also less competition from the crowds.

Most lakes are too small to generate enough wind to make waves. But there are some big exceptions. The Great Lakes, in the northern United States, are among the largest lakes in the world. There's enough wind there to generate waves, so surfing is possible. Another place is Lake Tahoe, located on the border between California and Nevada. Surfing on a lake has its own challenges because the waves die down more quickly. That means surfers may have to go out in the storm that's creating the waves—quickly, before they're gone!

Windsurfing can also be done on either oceans or lakes. In general, a smaller or protected body of water is a good place to start. The key is to get enough wind to sail, but not so much that it makes the craft too difficult to handle.

Water skiing and wakeboarding are two of the most versatile water sports. They harness the power of wind and water, but they don't rely on it entirely. Instead, these sports use man-made motor power. That means they can be done virtually anywhere—the ocean, rivers, lakes, and ponds. If you are just starting out, choose calm water with a fairly large area. That gives you plenty of room to mess up! Once you get better, you may want to add in tricks or jumps. Expert athletes are always adding a little more spin and a few more inches to some already amazing moves. In that case, you may need a place that has **buoys**, ramps, or cables.

Some people even do water sports inside. Many large cities have indoor water parks with artificial beaches and machines that produce surf. Water skiers and wakeboarders can practice in a pool. A motor pulls the skier or boarder one way, just like a boat would. Meanwhile,

Artificial surf breaks, such as this one on a cruise ship, take surfing away from the beach.

TRICKED OUT

One exciting trick in wakeboarding is called the layout, or "air Raley." In this trick, a wakeboarder lifts himself far out of the water, and throws his feet out behind and over him before coming back in for a landing. It looks kind of like a handstand in midair. Darin Shapiro is a professional wakeboarder from Florida. He often did this trick when he was wakeboarding from an overhead cable. Then his coach, Chet Raley, suggested he try it from a boat. This would be more difficult because Shapiro would not get the extra lift provided by the cable. He decided to try it anyway, and nailed it the first time! He named the new version of the trick after his coach.

jets of water produce a current that pushes the other direction. The result is that the rider stays in place, like on a treadmill. It's even possible to windsurf indoors. Athletes slide their windsurfing boards down a ramp into a huge, long pool. Giant fans provide the "wind."

To the Top

Some athletes really like to be at the top of their game. In water sports, this means how fast a windsurfer can take a slalom course, or how far a water skier can jump. It means how many tricks a wakeboarder can do, and how long a surfer can hold a wave. There are lots of events held all over the world that test these athletes' skills and abilities.

Surfing competitions are well established in the world of water sports. Surfers compete on shortboards and long ones, and on regular waves and big ones. They are judged on the height and difficulty of their waves, the length of their rides, and their style and technique. No two waves on the ocean are the same, so surfing competitions can be tricky. In fact, it's sometimes hard just to figure out when to hold them. Mavericks is the name of a big-wave surfing contest held in the winter, off the coast of San Francisco. The organizers watch and wait until the waves get big enough. When they think the time is right, competitors get a text message or an email. Then they have 24-48 hours to show up!

Eleven-time world champ Kelly Slater is probably the best surfer of all time.

Water ski races are a ballet among boats, skiers, and long wakes.

Water skiing competitions are divided into several categories. In jumping, a skier sails off a ramp and flies. It doesn't matter how good he looks—the whole idea is just to go far. In trick skiing, there's another component: style. Skiers are scored based on the numbers of tricks they do, as well as their overall difficulty. In barefoot water skiing, competitors are judged on how good their start is, the tricks they can do, and the length of time they can stay on their feet—they get one point for each second. Slalom water skiing is about **precision**. Skiers going about 35 miles (56 km) per hour must show total control as they zig-zag through a series of six buoys. Slalom skiers take the course several times, and each time is more difficult. The boat goes faster, and the rope gets shorter, making it more difficult to get around the buoys.

Wakeboarding competitions are all about the tricks. Competitors do jumps, board-grabs and aerial tricks in their routines. They are scored based on how many tricks they can do in a certain period of time—and of course, how well they pull them off. Several wakeboarding competitions are sponsored by the World Wakeboard Association, and there is also a Pro Wakeboard Tour with five events over the course of the season. Each event has its own winner. There is also a "King of Wake" that goes to whoever does the best overall.

Wakeboarders can do amazing aerial tricks at high speed.

43

OLYMPIC DREAMS?

Although water sports are popular all over the world, many of them are not included in the Olympics. Wakeboarding and water skiing do not qualify, because they use motors (boats or cables) for power. Surfing is under consideration to be added to the 2020 Olympics. However, some surfers think that the sport is too laid back for a formal competition like the Olympics. Windsurfing (pictured) is the exception. It has been an Olympic sport since 1984 for men and 1992 for women. It almost got replaced by kiteboarding for 2016, but at the last minute the committee members changed their minds and windsurfing got to stay.

Windsurfing competitors have a lot of options, too. Freestyle and wave competitions are judged based on sailors' overall skill, as well as how well they adapt to the water conditions. A few tricks don't hurt, either! Windsurfers who feel the need for speed can compete in a number of racing events.

It's a long road—and a lot of falls!—to the top, but most people aren't trying to win a medal. They don't need the biggest waves or the biggest air. They just want to get wet and have fun. Water sports are a great way to make sure those lazy days of summer don't get *too* lazy—and they make for great summer vacation stories, too!

TEXT-DEPENDENT QUESTIONS

1. How is surfing different on the east and west coasts?

2. What do athletes do in a slalom water skiing competition?

3. Why are water skiing and wakeboarding not in the Olympics?

RESEARCH PROJECT

Choose a water sport and research some of the competitions held for it. Find out what skills are important and how the events are judged.

Amazing Big-Wave Surfing Action from California

FIND OUT MORE

WEBSITES

www.usawaterski.org/
This site has information on skills and different types of water skiing and wakeboarding.

www.surfertoday.com/
Check out this site for articles on surfing and windsurfing, plus cool photos.

BOOKS

Gigliotti, Jim. *Water Sports*. Oxford, England: Raintree, 2015.

Kalman, Bobbie. *Extreme Wakeboarding*. St. Catherines, Ontario: Crabtree Publishing, 2006.

Poolos, Jaime. *Surfing and Windsurfing*. New York: Rosen Publishing, 2015.

Thompson, Luke. *Essential Water Skiing for Teens*. New York: Children's Press, 2006.

SERIES GLOSSARY OF KEY TERMS

bushcraft wilderness skills, named for the remote bush country of Australia

camouflage a pattern or disguise in clothing designed to make it blend into the surroundings

conservation the act of preserving or protecting, such as an environment or species

ecosystem the habitats of species and the ways that species interact with each other

friction the resistance that happens when two surfaces rub together

insulation protection from something, such as extreme hot or cold

layering adding layers of clothing to stay warm and removing layers to cool off.

rewilding returning to a more natural state

synthetic man-made, often to imitate a natural material

traction the grip or contact that an object has with another surface

wake the waves produced by the movement of a boat

INDEX

air Raley 40
barefoot water skiing 10
boots and bindings 32
driving a boat 22
choosing gear 28, 29
fins 30, 31
Great Lakes 38
Hawaii 8, 38
history 8, 9, 10
indoor pools 39
kiteboarding 9
materials of boards 31
Mavericks 41
Olympics 44
safety 12
sailboards 32, 33
Samuelson, Ralph 10
ski jumping 10
Slater, Kelly 41
stand-up paddleboards 24
surfing 8, 18, 19, 28, 29, 30, 38
turning 20, 21
wakeboarding 8, 11, 18, 20, 21, 28, 29, 39, 40, 43
water conditions 16, 17
water skiing 8, 9, 18, 19, 20, 21, 42
wetsuits 34, 38
windsurfing 9, 22, 23, 32, 33, 39, 40, 44

PHOTO CREDITS

(Dreamstime.com: DT. Dollarphoto.com: Dollar) Dmitry Tsetkov/DT 6; Dusan Kostic/DT 9; Maurie Hill/DT 10; Showfact/DT 12; Viatcheslav Dusaleev/DT 14; Casaalmare/DT 16; Rafael Ben-ari/DT 17; Paul Topp/DT 17; Tomas Del Amo/DT 19; Ahmad Faizal Yahya/DT 21; Susan Leggett/DT 22; Yanlev/Dollar 23; John Wollwerth/DT 24; Galina Barskaya/DT 26; Glen Gaffney/DT 29; Robwilson39/DT 30; Jana Lumley/DT 32; Pavol Stredansky/DT 33; Showface/DT 34; Fotosforthought/DT 36; Picturemakersllc/DT 38; Ruth Peterkin/DT 39; 40; Joseandres27/DT 41; Acceleratorhams/DT 42; Homydesign/DT 43; Forster/DPPI-SIPA 547/ Newscom 44.

ABOUT THE AUTHOR

Diane Bailey has written about 50 nonfiction books for kids and teens, on topics ranging from science to sports to celebrities. Diane also works as a freelance editor, helping authors who write novels for children and young adults. Diane has two sons and two dogs, and lives in Kansas.